ITALIAN COOKING

Food photography by Peter Barry
Incidental photography by FPG International
Recipes styled by Jacqueline Bellafontaine
Edited by Jillian Stewart
Designed by Claire Leighton

CLB 2707
© 1992 Colour Library Books Ltd, Godalming, Surrey, England.
All rights reserved.
This 1992 edition published by Crescent Books,
distributed by Outlet Book Company Inc., a Random House Company,
40 Engelhard Avenue, Avenel, New Jersey 07001.
Printed and bound in Singapore
ISBN 0 517 06599 1
8 7 6 5 4 3 2 1

ITALIAN COOKING

CRESCENT BOOKS
NEW YORK • AVENEL, NEW JERSEY

INTRODUCTION

Pasta and pizza – two of Italy's most famous exports – first introduced the world to the delights of Italian cooking. Pasta has been freshly made in Italian homes for generations, but the wide range of fresh pastas now available from delicatessens makes preparing the perfect pasta dish much easier. Naples has the distinction of inventing the pizza. Bakers rolled out their dough to make a thin base then covered it with a simple topping such as cheese and anchovies. Today's pizza is a much grander affair and the choice of toppings is as limitless as your imagination.

The huge increase in the number of people traveling to Italy on vacation means that a much wider range of traditional Italian food is becoming more widely known and loved. Dishes such as *gnocchi*, *polenta* and *risotto* have found their way into our Italian restaurants alongside sumptuous veal dishes and a bewildering array of exotic pasta recipes. In Italy cooking has always been regarded as a pleasure and a convivial atmosphere should be part of every Italian meal whether it is in your own kitchen or in the local trattoria!

Modern-day Italian cuisine has been shaped by many forces. Ancient Rome was once infamous for its exotic carnivorous feasts, but it is the food of the peasants which has endured through the ages. Simple dishes made from fresh local produce are still the backbone of good Italian cooking. The favorable climate, fertile land and proximity to the sea means that wheat, fruit and vegetables, and seafood are in abundant supply. And it is the quality and freshness of ingredients that are the crucial factors in the perfect Italian meal. Even today a surprising number of Italian households still grow their own vegetables and herbs to ensure the freshest possible ingredients. And for city dwellers shopping every day at a local market is the best way of ensuring good quality produce.

One of the great strengths of Italian cooking is its regional diversity. Each area of Italy has its own specialty; Apulia, for instance, is renowed for its seafood, while Umbria is home of the truffle. Rome is justly famous for cheeses such as Mozzarella and Ricotta, and Naples has the honor of producing some of the world's most delicious ice creams.

With such a wonderful culinary tradition, it is obvious that food is important to Italians. Mealtimes are a time for the family to get together, to chat, to relax and most of all to take time to enjoy their food. Italian meals are lengthy affairs be it at home or in a restaurant. An everyday meal will often consist of three courses, whereas a special occasion or family gathering involves such delights as soup, pasta, a meat dish, vegetables, risotto or polenta, and ice cream, fruit or cheese, and of course, wine!

With all these culinary delights to boast of it is little wonder that Italian cuisine is one of the world's favorites. So serve up a taste of Italian cooking and bring all the warmth and taste of this exciting cuisine into your home.

The narrow waterways of Venice (right) wind their way through the ancient city.

Melon and Prosciutto

Preparation Time: 20 minutes   **Serves:** 4

This is one of the best-loved Italian appetizers. It deserves to be, because the flavor of a ripe melon and the richness of Italian ham complement one another perfectly.

Ingredients
1 large ripe melon   16 thin slices prosciutto ham

Cut the melon in half lengthways, scoop out the seeds and discard them. Cut the melon into quarters and carefully pare off the rind. Cut each quarter into four slices. Wrap each slice of melon in a slice of prosciutto and place on a serving dish. Alternatively, place the melon slices on the dish and cover with the slices of prosciutto, leaving the ends of the melon showing. Serve immediately.

The bars, restaurants and cafes in the Piazza del Duomo in Milan make it a popular meeting place and the perfect spot to watch the world go by.

Minestrone

Preparation Time: 20 minutes **Cooking Time:** 2 hours **Serves:** 8-10

Everyone's favorite Italian soup doesn't always have to contain pasta. Our's substitutes potatoes and is hearty enough to serve as a meal.

Ingredients

8oz dried white cannellini beans
2 tbsps olive oil
1 large ham bone, preferably
    prosciutto
1 onion, chopped
2 cloves garlic, crushed
4 sticks celery, sliced
2 carrots, diced
1 small head Savoy cabbage or
    1lb fresh spinach, well washed
4oz green beans, cut into
    1 inch lengths
8oz tomatoes, peeled, seeded
    and diced
1 dried red chili pepper
10 cups water (or half beef stock)
Salt and pepper
1 sprig fresh rosemary
1 bay leaf
3 potatoes, peeled and cut
    into small dice
3 zucchini, trimmed and cut
    into small dice
1 tbsp chopped fresh basil
1 tbsp chopped fresh parsley
Grated Parmesan cheese
Salt and pepper

Place the beans in a large bowl, cover with cold water and leave to soak overnight. Heat the oil in a large stock pot and add ham bone, onion and garlic. Cook until onion has softened but not colored. Add the celery, carrots, cabbage and green beans. If using spinach, reserve until later.

Drain the beans and add them to the pot with the tomatoes and the chili pepper. Add the water and bring to the boil, skimming the surface as necessary. Add the rosemary and bay leaf and simmer, uncovered, until the beans are tender, about 1¼ hours. Add the potatoes and cook for the further 20 minutes. Add the zucchini and spinach and cook, skimming the surface, about 20 minutes longer. Remove the ham bone, rosemary and bay leaf and add basil and parsley. Serve with Parmesan cheese.

Spinach Gnocchi

Preparation Time: 15 minutes **Cooking Time:** 20 minutes **Serves:** 4-6

Gnocchi are dumplings that are served like pasta. A dish of gnocchi can be served as a first course or as a light main course, sprinkled with cheese or accompanied by a sauce.

Ingredients

4oz chopped, frozen spinach
8oz ricotta cheese
3oz Parmesan cheese
Salt and pepper

Freshly grated nutmeg
1 egg, slightly beaten
3 tbsps butter

Defrost the spinach and press it between two plates to extract all the moisture. Mix the spinach with the ricotta cheese, half the Parmesan cheese, salt, pepper and nutmeg. Gradually add the egg, beating well until the mixture holds together when shaped. With floured hands, shape the mixture into oval shapes. Use about 1 tbsp mixture for each gnocchi. Lower into simmering water, 3 or 4 at a time, and allow to cook gently until the gnocchi float to the surface, about 1-2 minutes. Remove with a draining spoon and place in a well buttered ovenproof dish.

When all the gnocchi are cooked, sprinkle on the remaining Parmesan cheese and dot with the remaining butter. Reheat 10 minutes in a hot oven and brown under a pre-heated broiler before serving.

The Colosseum in Rome was inaugurated by Titus in A.D. 80 and was the scene of numerous gladitorial contests between both men and beasts.

Bruschetta with Tomatoes

Preparation Time: 15 minutes **Cooking Time:** 25 minutes **Serves:** 6-8

Cooked over a wood fire in the traditional way, or more conveniently in the oven, tomatoes, basil and crisp bread make an unusual and informal starter.

Ingredients

18 slices of crusty Italian bread, cut 1 inch thick
2 cloves garlic, crushed
½ cup olive oil
Salt and pepper
18 large fresh basil leaves
4-5 ripe tomatoes, depending on size

Place the bread slices on a baking sheet and toast for about 10 minutes on each side at 375°F. Spread some of the garlic on both sides of each slice. Heat the oil gently in a small saucepan. Arrange the bread on a serving plate and immediately pour over the warm oil. Sprinkle with salt and pepper. Slice the tomatoes in ½ inch rounds. Place one basil leaf and one slice of tomato on each slice of bread and serve immediately.

A picturesque church huddles beneath Italy's Dolomite Mountains.

Tomato Salad Rustica

Preparation Time: 20 minutes **Cooking Time:** 30 minutes **Serves:** 4

An informal salad with a country flavor, this is perfect with barbecued meat, poultry or fish.

Ingredients

1lb tomatoes	2 tbsps capers
1 onion	1 tsp chopped fresh oregano or basil
4-6 anchovies	6 tbsps olive oil
Milk	1 tbsp lemon juice

Soak the anchovies in a little milk before using, rinse, pat dry and chop. Cut the tomatoes into quarters and remove the cores. Slice each quarter in half again and place them in a serving bowl. Slice the onion into rounds and then separate into rings. Scatter over the tomatoes. Cut the anchovies into small pieces and add to the tomatoes and onions along with the capers.

Mix the herbs, salt, pepper, oil and lemon juice together until well emulsified and pour over the salad. Mix all the ingredients gently and leave to stand for about 30 minutes before serving.

The most appropriate way to explore the beautiful city of Venice is by gondola.

Sicilian Caponata

Preparation Time: 30 minutes   **Cooking Time:** 25 minutes   **Serves:** 6

Vegetables, so important in Italian cuisine, are often served separately. This combination makes an excellent appetizer, vegetable course or accompaniment.

Ingredients

1 eggplant	1lb canned plum tomatoes
Salt	2 tbsps red wine vinegar
½ cup olive oil	1 tbsp sugar
1 onion, sliced	1 clove garlic, crushed
2 sweet red peppers, cored, seeded and cut into 1 inch pieces	12 black olives, pitted
	1 tbsp capers
2 sticks celery, sliced thickly	Salt and pepper

Cut the eggplant in half and score the cut surface. Sprinkle with salt and leave to drain in a colander or on paper towels for 30 minutes. Rinse, pat dry and cut into 1 inch cubes. Heat the oil in a large sauté pan and add the onion, peppers and celery. Lower the heat and cook for about 5 minutes, stirring occasionally. Add the eggplant and cook a further 5 minutes. Sieve the tomatoes to remove the seeds and add the pulp and liquid to the vegetables in the sauté pan. Add the remaining ingredients except the olives and capers and cook for a further 2 minutes.

To remove the stones from the olives, roll them on a flat surface to loosen the stones and then remove them with a swivel vegetable peeler. Alternatively, use a cherry pitter. Slice the olives in quarters and add to the vegetables with the capers. Simmer, uncovered, over moderate heat for 15 minutes to evaporate most of the liquid. Adjust the seasoning and serve hot or cold.

Miramare Castle near Trieste stands majestically on the point of a headland. The castle was built in 1860 for an Austrian archduke and his princess.

Flageolet, Tuna and Tomato Salad

Preparation Time: 15 minutes   **Serves:** 6-8

Tuna and tomatoes are two popular ingredients in Italian antipasto dishes. Add beans, with their pale green color, for an attractive and easy first course or salad.

Ingredients

1lb canned flageolet beans (substitute navy beans or butter beans)
6oz canned tuna in oil
Juice of 1 lemon

Chopped fresh herbs (parsley, oregano, basil or marjoram)
8 tbsps olive oil
Salt and pepper
6-8 tomatoes, sliced

Drain the beans, rinse and leave in a colander to dry. Drain the tuna and flake it into a bowl. Chop the herbs finely and mix with lemon juice, oil, salt and pepper. Add the beans to the tuna fish in the bowl and pour over the dressing, tossing carefully. Do not allow the tuna to break up too much. Adjust the seasoning and pile the salad into a mound in a shallow serving dish. Cut the tomatoes into rounds about ¼-inch thick and place against the mound of salad. Serve immediately.

The sophisticated resort of Rapallo is a popular destination for tourists.

Pepper Salad with Capers

Preparation Time: 30 minutes, 1 hour refrigeration **Serves:** 4-6

Capers, the flower buds of a plant that flourishes in the warm Italian climate, are a favorite ingredient in Italian cooking.

Ingredients

3 large peppers, red, green and yellow
6 tbsps olive oil
1 clove garlic, peeled and finely chopped

Basil leaves, roughly chopped
Fresh marjoram, roughly chopped
2 tbsps capers
1 tbsp white wine vinegar

Cut the peppers in half and remove the core and seeds. Press with the palm of the hand or the back of a knife to flatten. Brush the skin side with oil and place the peppers under a preheated broiler. Broil the peppers until the skins are well charred. Wrap in a towel and leave for 15 minutes. Unwrap and peel off the charred skin. Cut the peppers into thick strips and arrange on a serving dish. Scatter over the chopped garlic, basil leaves, marjoram and capers. Mix together the remaining olive oil with the vinegar and salt and pepper and pour over the salad. Refrigerate for 1 hour before serving.

The island of San Giorgio boasts the noble church of San Giorgio Maggiore, begun in 1566. The campanile is similar to its close neighbor in St. Mark's Square.

Pizza Rustica

Preparation Time: 40 minutes **Cooking Time:** 35 minutes **Serves:** 4-6

This farmhouse pie is really a cross between quiche and pizza. Whichever you think it resembles most, there is no question that it is delicious.

Ingredients
Pizza Dough
(see recipe for Pizza with Peppers, Olives and Anchovies)

Filling

Grated Parmesan cheese	1 tbsp chopped fresh basil
4oz prosciutto or Parma ham, sliced	2 eggs, lightly beaten
2 tomatoes, peeled, seeded and roughly chopped	5 tbsps heavy cream
2oz Mozzarella cheese, diced	2oz Fontina cheese, finely grated
1 tbsp chopped fresh parsley	Pinch nutmeg
	Salt and pepper

Prepare the dough as for the Pizza with Peppers, Olives and Anchovies. When the dough has doubled in bulk, knock it back and knead lightly. Flatten the dough into a circle or rectangle and roll out. Roll to a circle about 10 inches in diameter or a rectangle about 11 x 7 inches. Lightly oil the baking dish, place in the dough and press out with floured fingertips to form a raised edge on the sides of the dish. Sprinkle the base of the dough with some of the Parmesan cheese and place on a layer of ham. Cover the ham with the chopped tomato. Mix the remaining ingredients together and pour over the tomato and ham.

Bake on the lowest shelf of the oven for about 35 minutes at 375°F. The top of the pizza should be nicely browned and the edge of the dough should be golden when the pizza is ready. Serve hot.

Cemeteries dating from as far back as A.D. 2, line the Old Appian Way, in Rome.

Lasagne Napoletana

Preparation Time: 25 minutes **Cooking Time:** 1-1¼ hours **Serves:** 6

This is lasagne as it is cooked and eaten in Naples. With its layers of red, green and white it looks as delicious as it tastes and is very easy to prepare and assemble.

Ingredients
9 sheets spinach lasagne pasta

Tomato Sauce
3 tbsps olive oil
2 cloves garlic, crushed
2lbs fresh tomatoes, peeled, or
    canned tomatoes, drained

2 tbsps chopped fresh basil, six
    whole leaves reserved
Salt and pepper
Pinch sugar

Cheese Filling
1lb ricotta cheese
4 tbsps unsalted butter
8oz Mozzarella cheese, grated

Salt and pepper
Pinch nutmeg

Cook the pasta for 8 minutes in boiling salted water with 1 tbsp oil. Drain and rinse under hot water and place in a single layer on a damp cloth. Cover with another damp cloth and set aside. To prepare the sauce, cook the garlic in remaining oil for about 1 minute in a large saucepan. When pale brown, add the tomatoes, basil, salt, pepper and sugar. If using fresh tomatoes, drop into boiling water for 6-8 seconds. Transfer to cold water and leave to cool completely. This will make the peels easier to remove.

Lower the heat under the saucepan and simmer the sauce for 35 minutes. Add more seasoning or sugar to taste. Beat the ricotta cheese and butter together until creamy and stir into the remaining ingredients.

To assemble the lasagne, oil a rectangular baking dish and place 3 sheets of lasagne on the base. Cover with one third of the sauce and carefully spread on a layer of cheese. Place another 3 layers of pasta over the cheese and cover with another third of the sauce. Add the remaining cheese filling and cover with the remaining pasta. Spoon the remaining sauce on top. Cover with foil and bake for 20 minutes at 375°F. Uncover and cook for 10 minutes longer. Garnish with the reserved leaves and leave to stand 10-15 minutes before serving.

Crespelle alla Bolognese

Preparation Time: 45 minutes **Cooking Time:** 1¼ hours **Serves:** 6-8

Bolognese Filling

2 tbsps butter or margarine
1 tbsp olive oil
2 onions, finely chopped
8oz minced beef
1 small green pepper, seeded,
    cored and finely chopped
4oz canned plum tomatoes

1 tbsp tomato purée
½ cup beef stock
1 bay leaf
2 tsps chopped basil
1 tsp chopped oregano
2 tbsps sherry
Salt and pepper

Crespelle Batter

3 eggs
1 cup all-purpose flour
Pinch salt

1 cup water
2 tsps olive oil
Melted butter

Tomato sauce

1 tbsp butter or margarine
1 clove garlic, crushed
1 onion, finely chopped

1lb canned plum tomatoes
Salt, pepper and a pinch of sugar
Fresh basil leaves

Heat the butter and oil in a deep saucepan for the Bolognese filling. Put in the onion and cook slowly until soft but not colored. Increase the heat and add the beef. Stir the beef while cooking until all the meat is brown. Add chopped pepper, tomatoes and their juice, tomato purée, stock, herbs, salt and pepper to taste and simmer gently for about 45 minutes or until the mixture thickens, stirring occasionally. Add the sherry and cook for a further 5 minutes and set aside. Sift the flour for the crespelle with a pinch of salt. Break the eggs into a bowl and beat to mix thoroughly. Mix the flour into the eggs gradually, beating all the time until the mixture is smooth. Add water and the oil and stir in well. Cover the bowl with a damp cloth and leave in a cool place for 30 minutes.

Heat the crêpe pan or a 7 inch frying pan. Lightly grease with the melted butter and pour a large spoonful of the batter into the center of the pan. Swirl the pan to coat the base evenly. Fry until the crespelle is brown on the underside, loosen the edge with a palette knife, and turn over and brown the other side. Stack and wrap in a clean towel until needed.

To make the tomato sauce, melt butter in a small saucepan and cook garlic and onion slowly for about 5 minutes, or until softened but not colored. Reserve whole basil leaves for garnish and chop 2 tsps. Add the tomatoes to the onions and garlic along with the basil, salt, pepper and a pinch of sugar. Cook for about 10-15 minutes or until the onions are completely soft. Drain to remove the seeds, pressing the pulp against the strainer to extract the liquid.

Put 2 heaped spoonfuls of Bolognese filling into each crespelle. Roll up and place in an ovenproof dish. Repeat until all crespelles have been filled. Put into a 400°F oven and heat for 8 minutes. Heat the tomato sauce and spoon over the crespelle before serving. Garnish with basil leaves and serve.

Penne with Ham and Asparagus

Preparation Time: 20 minutes **Cooking Time:** 10-20 minutes **Serves:** 4

The Italian word penne means quills, due to the diagonal cut on both ends.

Ingredients

8oz penne
12oz fresh asparagus
4oz cooked ham

2 tbsps butter or margarine
1 cup heavy cream

Using a swivel vegetable peeler, scrape the sides of the asparagus spears starting about 2 inches from the top. Cut off the ends of the spears about 1 inch from the bottom. Cut the ham into strips about ½-inch thick.

Bring a sauté pan of water to the boil, adding a pinch of salt. Move the pan so it is half on and half off direct heat. Place in the asparagus spears so that the tips are off the heat. Cover the pan and bring back to the boil. Cook the asparagus spears for about 2 minutes. Drain and allow to cool. Cut the asparagus into 1 inch lengths, leaving the tips whole.

Melt the butter in the sauté pan and add the asparagus and ham. Cook briefly to evaporate the liquid, and add the cream. Bring to the boil and cook for about 5 minutes to thicken the cream.

Meanwhile, cook the pasta in boiling salted water with 1 tbsp oil for about 10-12 minutes. Drain the pasta and rinse under hot water. Toss in a colander to drain and mix with the sauce. Serve with grated Parmesan cheese, if desired.

Lipari is dominated by an imposing 16th-century castle and its ramparts.

Seafood Torta

Preparation Time: 35-40 minutes **Cooking Time:** 40 minutes **Serves:** 6-8

A very stylish version of a fish flan, this makes a perfect accompaniment to an Italian aperitif or serves as a light supper dish with salad.

Ingredients

Pastry
2 cups all-purpose flour, sifted
½ cup unsalted butter

Pinch salt
4 tbsps cold milk

Filling
4oz whitefish fillets (plaice,
    sole or cod)
8oz cooked shrimp
4oz flaked crab meat
½ cup white wine
½ cup water
Large pinch hot pepper flakes

Salt and pepper
2 tbsps butter
2 tbsps flour
1 clove garlic, crushed
2 egg yolks
½ cup heavy cream
Chopped fresh parsley

To prepare the pastry, sift the flour into a bowl or onto a work surface. Cut the butter into small pieces and begin mixing them into the flour. Mix until the mixture resembles fine breadcrumbs – this may also be done in a food processor. Make a well in the flour, pour in the milk and add the pinch of salt. Mix with a fork, gradually incorporating the butter and flour mixture from the sides until all the ingredients are mixed. This may also be done in a food processor. Form the dough into a ball and knead for about 1 minute. Leave the dough in the refrigerator for about 1 hour.

To prepare the filling, cook whitefish fillets in the water and wine with the red pepper flakes for about 10 minutes or until just firm to the touch. When the fish is cooked, remove it from the liquid and flake it into a bowl with the shrimp and the crab meat. Reserve the cooking liquid.

Melt the butter in a small saucepan and stir in the flour. Gradually strain on the cooking liquid from the fish, stirring constantly until smooth. Add garlic, place over high heat and bring to the boil. Lower the heat and allow to cook for 1 minute. Add to the fish in the bowl and set aside to cool. On a well-floured surface, roll out the pastry and transfer it with a rolling pin to a tart pan with a removable base. Press the dough into the pan and cut off any excess. Prick the pastry base lightly with a fork and place a sheet of wax paper inside. Fill with rice, dried beans or baking beans and chill for 30 minutes. Bake the pastry shell blind for 15 minutes in a 375°F oven.

While the pastry is baking, combine the egg yolks, cream and parsley and stir into the fish filling. Adjust the seasoning with salt and pepper. When the pastry is ready, remove the paper and beans and pour in the filling. Return the tart to the oven and bake for a further 25 minutes. Allow to cool slightly and then remove from the pan. Transfer to a serving dish and slice before serving.

Home-made Tagliatelle with Summer Sauce

Preparation Time: 30 minutes **Cooking Time:** 5-6 minutes **Serves:** 4

Pasta making is not as difficult as you might think. It is well worth it, too, because home-made pasta is in a class by itself.

Ingredients
Pasta Dough
1 cup all-purpose flour
1 cup bread flour
2 large eggs
2 tsps olive oil
Pinch salt

Sauce
1lb unpeeled tomatoes, seeded and cut into small dice
1 large green pepper, cored, seeded and cut in small dice
1 onion, cut in small dice
1 tbsp chopped fresh basil
1 tbsp chopped fresh parsley
2 cloves garlic, crushed
½ cup olive oil and vegetable oil mixed

Place the flours in a mound on a work surface and make a well in the center. Place the eggs, oil and salt in the center of the well. Using a fork, beat the ingredients in the center to blend them and gradually incorporate the flour from the outside edge. The dough may also be mixed in a food processor. When half the flour is incorporated, start kneading using the palms of the hands and not the fingers. This may also be done in a food processor. Cover the dough and leave it to rest for 15 minutes.

Divide the dough in quarters and roll out thinly with a rolling pin on a floured surface or use a pasta machine, dusting dough lightly with flour before rolling. If using a machine, follow the manufacturer's directions. Allow the sheets of pasta to dry for about 10 minutes on a floured surface or tea towels. Cut the sheets into strips about ¼ inch wide by hand or machine, dusting lightly with flour while cutting. Leave the cut pasta to dry while preparing the sauce. Combine all the sauce ingredients, mixing well. Cover and refrigerate overnight.

Cook the pasta for 5-6 minutes in boiling salted water with a spoonful of oil. Drain the pasta and rinse under very hot water. Toss in a colander to drain excess water. Place the hot pasta in serving dish. Pour the cold sauce over and toss.

Spaghetti Amatriciana

Preparation Time: 20-25 minutes **Cooking Time:** 10-20 minutes **Serves:** 4

This is another quickly cooked sauce with a rich spicy taste. Use less of the chili pepper for a less fiery flavor.

Ingredients

1 onion
6 strips smoked back bacon
1lb ripe tomatoes

1 red chili pepper
1½ tbsps oil
12oz spaghetti

Slice the onion thinly. Remove rind from the bacon and cut into thin strips. Drop the tomatoes into boiling water for 6-8 seconds. Remove with a draining spoon and place in cold water, and leave to cool completely. This will make the peels easier to remove. When the tomatoes are peeled, cut them in half and remove the seeds and pulp with a teaspoon. Rub the seeds and pulp through a strainer and retain juice to use in the sauce if desired. Chop the tomato flesh roughly and set it aside.

Cut the stem off the chili pepper and cut the pepper in half lengthways. Remove the seeds and core and cut the pepper into thin strips. Cut the strips into small dice.

Heat the oil in a sauté pan and add the onion and bacon. Stir over medium heat for about 5 minutes, until the onion is transparent. Drain off excess fat and add the tomatoes and chili and mix well. Simmer the sauce gently, uncovered, for about 5 minutes, stirring occasionally.

Meanwhile, cook the spaghetti in boiling salted water with 1 tbsp oil for about 10-12 minutes. Drain and rinse in hot water and toss in a colander to dry. To serve, spoon the sauce on top of the spaghetti and sprinkle with freshly grated Parmesan cheese, if desired.

Early morning in Verona and the cafes are ready for another busy day.

Spirali with Spinach and Bacon

Preparation Time: 20 minutes **Cooking Time:** 14-16 minutes **Serves:** 4

Pasta doesn't have to have a sauce that cooks for hours. This whole dish takes about 15 minutes. True Italian "fast food"!

Ingredients

12oz pasta spirals
8oz fresh spinach
3oz bacon
1 clove garlic, crushed
1 small red or green chili pepper

1 small red sweet pepper
1 small onion
3 tbsps olive oil
Salt and pepper

Cook the pasta in boiling salted water about 10-12 minutes or until just tender. Drain the pasta in a colander and rinse it under hot water. Keep the pasta in a bowl of water until ready to use. Tear the stalks off the spinach and wash the leaves well, changing the water several times. Set aside to drain. Remove the rind and bones from the bacon, if necessary, and dice the bacon finely. Cut the chili and the red pepper in half, remove the stems, core and seed and slice finely. Slice the onion thinly. Roll up several of the spinach leaves into a cigar shape and then shred them finely. Repeat until all the spinach is shredded. Heat the oil in a sauté pan and add garlic, onion, peppers and bacon. Fry for 2 minutes, add the spinach and fry for a further 2 minutes, stirring continuously. Season with salt and pepper. Drain the pasta spirals and toss them in a colander to remove excess water. Mix with the spinach sauce and serve immediately.

The Amalfi coast is one of Italy's most beautiful regions.

Pizza with Peppers, Olives & Anchovies

Preparation Time: 40 minutes **Cooking Time:** 20-30 minutes **Serves:** 4

Pizza really needs no introduction. It originated in Naples and has been adopted everywhere. Change the toppings to suit your taste.

Ingredients
Pizza Dough
½oz fresh yeast
½tsp sugar
¾cup lukewarm water

2 cup all-purpose flour
Pinch salt
2 tbsps oil

Topping
2 tsps olive oil
1 onion, finely chopped
1 clove garlic, crushed
1lb canned tomatoes
1 tbsp tomato purée
½tsp each oregano and basil
1 tsp sugar

Salt and pepper
½red pepper
½green pepper
2oz black olives, pitted
2oz canned anchovies, drained
4oz Mozzarella cheese, grated
2 tbsp grated Parmesan cheese

Cream the yeast with the sugar in a small bowl, add the lukewarm water and leave to stand for 10 minutes to prove. Bubbles will appear on the surface when ready. Sift flour and salt into a bowl, make a well in the center, add the oil and the yeast mixture. Using a wooden spoon, beat the liquid in the center of the well, gradually incorporating the flour from the outside until it forms a firm dough. Turn the dough out onto a floured surface and knead for 10 minutes or until the dough is smooth and elastic. Place in a lightly oiled bowl or in a large plastic bag, cover or tie the bag and leave to stand in a warm place for 30 minutes, or until the dough has doubled in bulk. Knock the dough back and knead it into a smooth ball. Flatten the dough and roll out into a circle on a floured surface. The circle should be about 10 inches in diameter.

To prepare the topping, heat the oil in a heavy-based saucepan and add the onion and the garlic. Cook until the onion and garlic have softened but not colored. Add the tomatoes and their juice, tomato purée, herbs, sugar, salt and pepper. Bring the sauce to the boil and then allow to simmer, uncovered, to reduce. Stir the sauce occasionally to prevent sticking. When the sauce is thick and smooth, leave it to cool. Spread the cooled sauce over the pizza dough. Sprinkle half the cheese on top of the tomato sauce and then arrange the topping ingredients. Sprinkle with remaining cheese and bake in a 400°F oven for 15-20 minutes or until the cheese is melted and bubbling and the crust is brown.

Swordfish Kebabs

Preparation Time: 15 minutes **Cooking Time:** 10 minutes **Serves:** 4-6

Swordfish is one of the most commonly caught fish in Southern Italy and Sicily. It won't fall apart during cooking – a bonus when making kebabs.

Ingredients

2¼ lbs swordfish steaks
6 tbsps olive oil
1 tsp chopped oregano
1 tsp chopped marjoram
Juice and rind of ½ a lemon

4 tomatoes, cut in thick slices
2 lemons, cut in thin slices
Salt and freshly ground pepper
Lemon slices and Italian parsley
   for garnish

Cut the swordfish steaks into 2 inch pieces. Mix the olive oil, herbs, lemon juice and rind together and set it aside. Thread the swordfish, tomato slices and lemon slices on skewers, alternating the ingredients. Brush the skewers with the oil and lemon juice mixture and cook under a preheated broiler for about 10 minutes, basting frequently with the lemon and oil. Serve garnished with lemons and parsley.

The Forum is the center of old Rome and gives a fascinating insight into the architecture of the ancient city.

Fish Milanese

Preparation Time: 1 hour **Cooking Time:** 6 minutes **Serves:** 4

These fish, cooked in the style of Milan, have a crispy crumb coating and the fresh tang of lemon juice.

Ingredients

8 sole or plaice fillets
2 tbsps dry vermouth
1 bay leaf
6 tbsps olive oil
Salt and pepper
Seasoned flour for dredging
2 eggs, lightly beaten
Dry breadcrumbs
Oil for shallow frying

6 tbsps butter
1 clove garlic, crushed
2 tsps chopped parsley
2 tbsps capers
1 tsp chopped fresh oregano
Juice of 1 lemon
Salt and pepper
Lemon wedges and parsley to garnish

Skin the fillets with a sharp filleting knife. Remove any small bones and place the fillets in a large, shallow dish. Combine the vermouth, oil and bay leaf in a small saucepan and heat gently. Allow to cool completely and pour over the fish. Leave the fish to marinate for about 1 hour, turning them occasionally. Remove the fish from the marinade and dredge lightly with the seasoned flour. Dip the fillets into the beaten eggs to coat, or use a pastry brush to brush the eggs onto the fillets. Dip the egg-coated fillet into the breadcrumbs, pressing the crumbs on firmly.

Heat the oil in a large frying pan. Add the fillets and cook slowly on both sides until golden brown. Cook for about 3 minutes on each side, remove and drain on paper towels. Pour the oil out of the frying pan and wipe it clean. Add the butter and the garlic and cook until both turn a light brown. Add the herbs, capers and lemon juice and pour immediately over the fish. Garnish with lemon wedges and sprigs of parsley.

Sunbathers find the perfect location near the old town of Polignano a Mare.

Red Mullet with Herb & Mushroom Sauce

Preparation Time: 30 minutes **Cooking Time:** 25 minutes **Serves:** 4

This is a Mediterranean fish with a slight taste of shrimp. It is often cooked with the liver left in – a delicacy.

Ingredients

1lb small mushrooms, left whole
1 clove garlic, finely chopped
3 tbsps olive oil
Juice of 1 lemon
1 tbsp finely chopped parsley
2 tsps finely chopped basil
1 tsp finely chopped marjoram
  or sage
4 tbsps dry white wine mixed
  with ½tsp cornstarch
Few drops anchovy essence
4 red mullet, each weighing
  about 8oz
2 tsps white breadcrumbs
2 tsps freshly grated Parmesan
  cheese

Combine the mushrooms, garlic and olive oil in a small frying pan. Cook over moderate heat for about 1 minute, until the garlic and mushrooms are slightly softened. Add all the herbs, lemon juice and white wine and cornstarch mixture. Bring to the boil and cook until thickened. Add anchovy essence to taste. Set aside while preparing the fish. To clean the fish, cut along the stomach from the gills to the vent, the small hole near the tail. Clean out the cavity of the fish, leaving the liver, if desired. To remove the gills, lift the flap and snip them out with a sharp pair of scissors. Rinse the fish well and pat dry. Place the fish head to tail in a shallow ovenproof dish that can be used for serving. The fish should fit snugly into the dish.

Pour the prepared sauce over the fish and sprinkle with the breadcrumbs and Parmesan cheese. Cover the dish loosely with foil and cook in the preheated oven 375°F, for about 20 minutes. Uncover for the last 5 minutes, if desired, and raise the oven temperature slightly. This will lightly brown the fish.

The Gianicolo Hill gives a panoramic view of clouds gathering over Rome.

Turkey Kebabs

Preparation Time: 20 minutes **Cooking Time:** 40 minutes **Serves:** 6

You don't have to buy a whole turkey for these! Small portions are now readily available at supermarkets.

Ingredients

3lbs turkey meat
2 tsps chopped sage
1 sprig rosemary
Juice of 1 lemon
2 tbsps olive oil

Salt and pepper
4oz streaky bacon, rinds and
   bones removed
Whole sage leaves

Remove any bones from the turkey and cut the meat into even-sized pieces. Combine the chopped sage, rosemary, lemon juice, oil, salt and pepper in a large bowl and add the turkey meat. Stir once or twice to coat evenly, cover and leave in the refrigerator overnight. Cut the bacon in half and wrap around some of the pieces of turkey. Leave other pieces of turkey unwrapped. Thread the bacon, wrapped turkey, plain turkey and whole sage leaves onto skewers, alternating the ingredients. Cook in a preheated 400°F oven for about 40 minutes. Alternatively, cook for 30 minutes and place the kebabs under a preheated broiler for 10 minutes to crisp the bacon. Baste frequently with the marinade while cooking. Pour any remaining marinade and pan juices over the kebabs to serve.

The Roman Forum was once the political and commercial center of ancient Rome.

Liver Veneziana

Preparation Time: 30 minutes **Cooking Time:** 4 minutes **Serves:** 4-6

As the name indicates, this recipe originated in Venice. The lemon juice offsets the rich taste of liver in this very famous Italian dish.

Ingredients
Risotto
9oz Italian rice
3 tbsps butter or margarine
1 large onion, chopped
4 tbsps dry white wine

2 cups chicken stock
¼ tsp saffron
2 tbsps grated fresh Parmesan cheese
Salt and pepper

Liver
1lb calves' or lambs' liver
Flour for dredging
3 onions, thinly sliced
2 tbsps butter or margarine

3 tbsps oil
Salt and pepper
Juice of ½ a lemon
1 tbsp chopped parsley

Melt the butter for the risotto in a large sauté pan, add the onion and cook until soft but not colored, over gentle heat. Add the rice and cook for about a minute until the rice looks clear. Add the wine, stock, saffron and seasoning. Stir well and bring to the boil. Lower the heat and cook gently, stirring frequently until the liquid has evaporated. This will take about 20 minutes. Meanwhile, skin the liver and cut out any large tubes. Cut the liver into strips and toss in a sieve with the flour to coat.

Heat the butter or margarine and 1 tbsp oil in a large sauté or frying pan. Cook the onions until golden. Remove the onions from the pan to a plate. Add more oil if necessary, raise the heat under the pan and add the liver. Cook, stirring constantly, for about 2 minutes. Return the onions and add the lemon juice and parsley. Cook a further 2 minutes or until the liver is done. Season with salt and pepper and serve with the risotto. To finish the risotto, add the cheese and salt and pepper to taste when the liquid has evaporated and toss to melt the cheese.

Veal Scaloppine with Prosciutto and Cheese

Preparation Time: 15 minutes **Cooking Time:** 15-20 minutes **Serves:** 4

Veal is the meat used most often in Italian cooking. Good veal is tender and quick cooking, but expensive. Save this recipe for your next dinner party!

Ingredients

8 veal escalopes
2 tbsps butter or margarine
1 clove garlic, crushed
1 sprig rosemary
8 slices prosciutto ham

8 slices Mozzarella cheese
3 tbsps sherry
½ cup beef stock
Salt and pepper

Pound the veal escalopes out thinly between two pieces of wax paper with a meat mallet or a rolling pin. Melt the butter or margarine in a sauté pan and add the veal and garlic. Cook until the veal is lightly browned on both sides.

Place a piece of prosciutto on top of each piece of veal and add the sherry, stock and sprig of rosemary to the pan. Cover the pan and cook the veal for about 10 minutes over gentle heat or until done. Remove the meat to a heatproof serving dish and top each piece of veal with a slice of cheese. Bring the cooking liquid from the veal to the boil and allow to boil rapidly to reduce slightly.

Meanwhile, grill the veal to melt and brown the cheese. Remove the sprig of rosemary from the sauce and pour the sauce around the meat to serve.

The Carabinieri are only one of three national police forces in Italy. Their origins are military and recruits still wear military-style uniform.

Pork Roulades with Polenta

Preparation Time: 20 minutes **Cooking Time:** 1 hour 40 minutes **Serves:** 4-8

Polenta, either boiled or fried, is a staple dish in Italy.

Ingredients

8oz coarse yellow cornmeal
6 cups chicken stock

Salt and white pepper

Roulades

8 pork escalopes or steaks
8 slices Parma ham
4 large cup mushrooms
4 tbsps grated Parmesan cheese
1 tbsp chopped fresh sage
Seasoned flour for dredging
4 tbsps olive oil
1 small onion, finely chopped
2 sticks celery, finely chopped

1 clove garlic, crushed
6 tbsps brown stock
½ cup dry white wine
4oz canned plum tomatoes, drained
    and juice reserved
1 tsp tomato purée
Salt and pepper
6 tbsps dry Marsala
Fresh sage leaves for garnish

Bring the chicken stock for the polenta to the boil in a large stock pot and start adding the cornmeal in a very slow, steady stream, stirring continuously. Add salt and pepper and continue cooking over very low heat, stirring frequently for about 55 minutes. Flatten the pork escalopes or steaks and place a slice of Parma ham on top of each. Chop the mushrooms and divide among the pork escalopes, spooning on top of the ham slices. Sprinkle over the Parmesan cheese and the fresh sage. Fold the sides of the pork escalopes into the center to seal them, and roll up the pork like a Swiss roll. Secure each roll with a toothpick. Dredge each roulade in flour, shaking off the excess.

Heat the olive oil in a large sauté pan of frying pan and add the pork roulades, seam side down first. Cook on all sides until nicely browned. Remove the roulades and keep them warm.

Add the onion and celery to the oil in the pan and cook until lightly browned. Add the garlic and all the remaining ingredients except the Marsala. Reserve the juice from the tomatoes for later use if necessary. Bring the sauce to the boil, breaking up the tomatoes. Return the roulades to the pan, cover and cook over moderate heat for about 15-20 minutes or until the pork is completely cooked. Add reserved tomato juice, as necessary, if liquid is drying out. When the pork is cooked, remove to a dish and keep it warm. Add the Marsala to the sauce and bring to the boil. Allow to boil 5-10 minutes. The sauce may be puréed in a food processor and also sieved if desired.

To assemble the dish, spoon the polenta onto a serving plate. Remove the toothpicks from the roulades and place on top of the polenta. Spoon the sauce over the meat and garnish the dish with fresh sage leaves.

Chicken Cacciatore

Preparation Time: 25-30 minutes **Cooking Time:** 1 hour 15 minutes **Serves:** 4-6

The name means Chicken the Hunter's Way, and that means the addition of mushrooms. Though not traditional, pasta is a good accompaniment.

Ingredients

3 tbsps oil
4oz mushrooms, quartered, if large
3lb chicken, skinned if desired
  and cut into pieces
1 onion
2 cloves garlic
½ cup vermouth
1 tbsp white wine vinegar
½ cup chicken stock
1 tsp oregano
1 sprig fresh rosemary
1lb canned tomatoes
2oz black olives, pitted
2 tbsps chopped parsley
Salt and pepper

Heat the oil in a heavy-based frying pan and cook the mushrooms for about 1-2 minutes. Remove them and set aside. Brown the chicken in the oil and transfer the browned pieces to an ovenproof casserole. Chop the onion and garlic finely. Pour off all but 1 tbsp of the oil in the frying pan and reheat the pan. Cook the onion and garlic until softened but not colored. Add the vermouth and vinegar and boil to reduce by half. Add the chicken stock, tomatoes, oregano, rosemary, salt and pepper. Break up the tomatoes and bring the sauce to the boil. Allow to cook for 2 minutes. Pour the sauce over the chicken in the casserole, cover and cook at 350°F for about 1 hour.

To remove the stones from the olives, roll them on a flat surface to loosen the stones and then use a swivel vegetable peeler to extract them. Alternatively use a cherry pitter. Add mushrooms and olives during the last 5 minutes of cooking. Remove the rosemary before serving and sprinkle with chopped parsley.

The charming village of Poggio is typical of the small island of Elba.

Turkey Marsala

Preparation Time: 35 minutes **Cooking Time:** 15 minutes **Serves:** 4

Marsala is a dessert wine from Sicily which also complements chicken, veal or turkey surprisingly well. It is traditional, but sherry will serve as a substitute if Marsala is unavailable.

Ingredients

4 turkey breast fillets or escalopes
4 tbsps butter or margarine
1 clove garlic
4 anchovy fillets, soaked in milk
Capers
4 slices Mozzarella cheese

2 tsps chopped marjoram
1 tbsp chopped parsley
3 tbsps Marsala
½ cup heavy cream
Salt and pepper

Flatten the turkey breasts between two sheets of wax paper with a meat mallet or rolling pin if necessary. Melt butter in a sauté pan and, when foaming, add the garlic and the turkey. Cook for a few minutes on each side until lightly browned. Remove them from the pan. Drain the anchovy fillets and rinse them well. Dry on paper towels. Put a slice of cheese on top of each turkey fillet and arrange the anchovies and capers on top of each. Sprinkle with the chopped herbs and return the turkey to the pan. Cook the turkey a further 5 minutes over moderate heat, until the turkey is done and the cheese has melted. Remove to a serving dish and keep warm. Return the pan to the heat and add the Marsala. Scrape the browned pan juices off the bottom and reduce the heat. Add the cream and whisk in well. Lower the heat and simmer gently, uncovered, for a few minutes to thicken the sauce. Season the sauce with salt and pepper and spoon over the turkey fillets to serve.

Each summer the resort of Sorrento plays host to a fleet of visiting yachts.

Caramel Oranges

Preparation Time: 25 minutes **Cooking Time:** 20-25 minutes **Serves:** 4

This is one of the classic Italian sweets. Vary the darkness of the caramel to suit your taste, but watch it carefully!

Ingredients

4 large oranges
1¼ cups sugar
1½ cups water

¼ cup extra water
2 tbsps brandy or orange liqueur

Use a swivel vegetable peeler to peel thin strips from two of the oranges. Take off any white pith and cut the strips into very thin julienne strips with a sharp knife. Place the julienne strips in a small saucepan, cover with water and bring to the boil.

Peel all the oranges with a serrated-edged knife. Cut the ends off first and then take the peel and pith off in very thin strips using a sawing motion. Cut the oranges horizontally into slices about ¼-inch thick. Drain the orange peel strips and leave to dry. Combine sugar and water in a heavy-based pan. Reserve ¼ cup water for later use. Place the mixture over medium heat until the sugar has dissolved. Add the drained orange peel strips to the pan. Boil the syrup gently, uncovered, for about 10 minutes or until the orange strips are glazed. Remove the strips from the pan and place on a lightly oiled plate.

Return the pan to high heat and allow the syrup to boil, uncovered, until it turns a pale golden brown. Remove from the heat immediately and quickly add the extra water. Return to gentle heat and cook for a few minutes to dissolve hardened sugar. Remove the pan from the heat and allow to cool completely. Stir in the brandy. Arrange the orange slices in a serving dish and pour over the cooled syrup. Pile the glazed orange strips on top and refrigerate for several hours, or overnight, before serving.

The old town of Monte Sant'Angelo in the southern region of Apulia.

Chestnut & Almond Stuffed Peaches

Preparation Time: 40 minutes   **Serves:** 4-8

A favorite sweet in Milan during the peach season, this recipe combines the sunny peach flavor with a luxurious chocolate and chestnut cream.

Ingredients
4 large freestone peaches
1 cup dry white wine

2 tbsps brandy

Filling
2oz semi-sweet chocolate
2¾ oz chestnut spread
1 egg yolk
1 tbsp ground almonds

1 tbsp peach liqueur or brandy
½ cup heavy cream
4 amaretti or ratafia biscuits

Wash the peaches, peel them and cut them in half. Carefully remove the stones and place the peaches in a large bowl with the wine, brandy and enough water to cover them completely. Marinate for 1 hour.

Cut the chocolate into small pieces and melt in the top of a double boiler. Stir in the chestnut spread. Remove the chocolate from the heat and leave to cool for about 2 minutes, stirring frequently. Beat in the egg yolk until well incorporated. Add the peach liqueur or brandy and stir well. Allow to cool.

Whip the cream and fold into the chocolate-chestnut mixture with the ground almonds. Allow to cool completely before using. Remove the peaches from the marinade with a draining spoon and place them in serving dishes. Fill a piping bag fitted with a large rosette nozzle with the chocolate-chestnut mixture. Pipe out a large rosette of chocolate-chestnut mixture into the hollow of each peach half. Place a biscuit on top of each peach and serve chilled, with cream if desired.

Zuppa Inglese

Preparation Time: 20 minutes **Cooking Time:** 15 minutes **Serves:** 6-8

This is Italy's tribute to trifle. The name means English soup, but the custard is rich and thick.

Ingredients

2 tbsps cornstarch	Pinch nutmeg
2 cups milk	1 punnet ripe strawberries
2 eggs, lightly beaten	16 sponge fingers
2 tbsps sugar	Amaretto
Grated rind of ½ a lemon	½ cup heavy cream

Mix the cornstarch with some of the milk. Beat the eggs, sugar lemon rind and nutmeg together and pour in the remaining milk. Mix with the cornstarch mixture in a heavy-based pan and stir over gentle heat until the mixture thickens and comes to the boil. Allow to boil for 1 minute or until the mixture coats the back of a spoon. Place a sheet of wax paper directly on top of the custard and allow it to cool slightly.

Save 8 even-sized strawberries for garnish and hull the remaining ones. Place half of the sponge fingers in the bottom of a glass bowl and sprinkle with some of the amaretto. Cut the strawberries in half and place a layer on top of the sponge fingers. Pour a layer of custard on top and repeat with the remaining sliced strawberries and sponge fingers. Top with another layer of custard and allow to cool completely.

Whip the cream and spread a thin layer over the top of the set custard. Pipe the remaining cream around the edge of the dish and decorate with the reserved strawberries. Serve chilled.

In Rome numerous luxury shops satisfy the Italian sense of style.

Cassata

Preparation Time: 2-3 hours   **Serves:** 6-8

No sweet selection is complete without ice cream. The Italian kind is rich, creamy and justly famous.

Ingredients
Almond Layer
2 eggs, separated
½ cup powdered sugar

½ cup heavy cream
½ tsp almond essence

Chocolate Layer
2 eggs, separated
½ cup powdered sugar
½ cup heavy cream

2oz semi-sweet chocolate
2 tbsps cocoa
1½ tbsps water

Fruit Layer
1 cup heavy cream
2 tbsps maraschino or light rum
1 egg white

½ cup powdered sugar
2oz mixed glacé fruit
1oz shelled chopped pistachios

To prepare the almond layer, beat egg whites until stiff peaks form, gradually beating in the powdered sugar, a spoonful at a time. Lightly beat the egg yolks and fold in the whites. Whip the cream with the almond essence until soft peaks form and fold into the egg mixture. Lightly oil a 8 inch round cake pan. Pour in the almond layer mixture and smooth over the top. Cover with plastic wrap and freeze until firm.

To prepare the chocolate layer, beat the egg whites until stiff but not dry and gradually beat in the powdered sugar. Whip the cream until soft and fold into the egg white mixture. Put the chocolate in the top of a double boiler over simmering water. Remove it from the heat and stir in the egg yolks. Combine cocoa and water and add to the chocolate mixture. Allow to cool and then fold into the egg white mixture. Spoon the chocolate layer over the almond layer and return, covered, to the freezer.

To make the rum fruit layer, whip the cream until soft peaks form. Whip the egg white until about the same consistency as cream. Gradually add the powdered sugar, beating well after each addition. Combine the two mixtures, fold in the rum, fruit and nuts. Spread this mixture on top of the chocolate layer, cover and freeze until firm.

To serve, loosen the cassata from around the edges of the pan with a small knife. Place a hot cloth around the pan for a few seconds to help loosen. Turn out onto a serving plate and cut into wedges to serve.

Appetizers:
    Bruschetta with Tomatoes 18
    Melon and Prosciutto 12
    Minestrone 14
    Spinach Gnocchi 16
Bruschetta with Tomatoes 18
Caramel Oranges 64
Cassata 70
Chestnut and Almond Stuffed Peaches 66
Chicken Cacciatore 60
Crespelle alla Bolognese 32
Desserts:
    Caramel Oranges 64
    Cassata 70
    Chestnut and Almond Stuffed Peaches 66
    Zuppa Inglese 68
Fish and Seafood:
    Fish Milanese 48
    Red Mullet with Herb and Mushroom
        Sauce 50
    Seafood Torta 36
    Swordfish Kebabs 46
Fish Milanese 48
Flageolet, Tuna and Tomato Salad 24
Home-made Tagliatelle with Summer Sauce 38
Lasagne Napoletana 30
Liver Veneziana 54
Meat and Poultry:
    Chicken Cacciatore 60
    Crespelle alla Bolognese 32
    Liver Veneziana 54
    Pork Roulades with Polenta 58
    Turkey Marsala 62
    Turkey Kebabs 52
    Veal Scaloppine with Prosciutto and
        Cheese 56

Melon and Prosciutto 12
Minestrone 14
Pasta:
    Home-made Tagliatelle with Summer
        Sauce 38
    Lasagne Napoletana 30
    Penne with Ham and Asparagus 34
    Spaghetti Amatriciana 40
    Spirali with Spinach and Bacon 42
Penne with Ham and Asparagus 34
Pepper Salad with Capers 26
Pizza:
    Pizza Rustica 28
    Pizza with Peppers, Olives and
        Anchovies 44
Pizza Rustica 28
Pizza with Peppers, Olives and Anchovies 44
Pork Roulades with Polenta 58
Red Mullet with Herb and Mushroom Sauce 50
Seafood Torta 36
Sicilian Caponata 22
Spaghetti Amatriciana 40
Spinach Gnocchi 16
Spirali with Spinach and Bacon 42
Swordfish Kebabs 46
Tomato Salad Rustica 20
Turkey Kebabs 52
Turkey Marsala 62
Veal Scaloppine with Prosciutto and
    Cheese 56
Vegetable and Side Dishes:
    Flageolet, Tuna and Tomato Salad 24
    Pepper Salad with Capers 26
    Sicilian Caponata 22
    Tomato Salad Rustica 20
Zuppa Inglese 68